Millionaire Mindset

Law of Attracting Wealth

JASON MARK

Table of Contents

Contents

Introduction

The whole world, including yourself, is seeking out on how to get rich faster and easier. How are we not going to fault ourselves on this? Who would not want to get rich easily and quickly? For as far as people are continuously seeking out to get rich easier, there have been lots of opportunists who take advantage of our aspirations and dreams, turning it into a disbelief of financial reality.

How can I become rich quickly? It is a very common question by most people every single day. Wealth is indeed among the most popular preoccupations by people these days. It may sound like a terrible thing but it is actually not. Money is important to be able to for us to live our life with comfort and to the fullest, and whether we like it or not, it is always going to have a huge part to play to help us reach our dreams.

If you want become rich easily and fast, among the options or reasons is when you have rich parents or grandparents. Nevertheless, if you do not have such things, you will have to start things from scratch, and it is something better, as you will be the one to turn yourself into a wealthy guy and not someone else. You will have to keep in mind that attaining wealth necessitates you to work hard. There is no such thing as teleportation into riches overnight. Look at various ways that this book share with you, along with the mistakes to avoid.

Chapter 1: How to Know if you are Rich

Perhaps you are thinking that being rich means being in the top of earners in some of the richest cities in the country, or in the world. Perhaps being rich means having the capability to purchase a flashy mansion or spending your life having to flit from one luxury vacation to another. However, being wealthy can be as subjective as being happy. Richness has difference for everyone. But there are several indications that you are rich, no matter how you see it.

You can live below your means comfortably

Among the main tenets of responsible money management is to live below your means. This means spending less than what you earn no matter how much it may be. Learning to live within your means and this will help you survive and flourish in your living means and business. You should have a discipline to make sure that the company you are working at, or your own company, and you, will not overspend.

Having to live within your means might not sound like a big deal if you have been doing it already, but not all people would be able to manage it. More than half of the thousands of Americans surveyed said that they are spending more than how much they earn, or they just break even every month.

You are not purely motivated by money

One usual thread that you will find among self-made millionaires, along with those who study them is that wealthy people tend to put their focus on something aside from the dollar sign. They solve a problem, they follow a passion, and they strive to build their business further as much as possible. It is a luxury and if you cannot make ends meet, you may bet that you are going to focus on the dollar signs than thinking of the intellectual fulfillment of your job.

It does not mean that you would not be able to be happy earning a sizable paycheck or that you are not going to be excite in watching your investments grow. Nonetheless, money is not your source of joy or best motivator. If you have that luxury to put your focus on other things aside from money, then you are in a good place.

You can save money

Most people do not realize that it is not how much money you make in life, but about how much money you are able to keep. At the end of the day, money will not be able to solve your financial problems. As a matter of fact, it usually exacerbates them, just like lottery winners who lost all of it within a few years, or the expert athletes who have made millions during their 20s but then wound up broke before they even retire.

Money usually makes out tragic human flaws obvious, and it puts a spotlight on the things that we do not know. This is the reason why people who come into a sudden windfall of cash returns to the same financial mess soon as compared to what they have been in before they get a lottery winnings, inheritance, or a pay raise. If you can hold on to a part of money that you earn, you are in good shape.

You can afford to retire as planned

It is expensive to retire. Professionals say that to be able to live in retirement lavishly, you will have to replace around 70 to 80 percent of your present income, even though that number is disputed. Even if you have been downsized, and perhaps even relocated to a place that has a low cost of living, retiring has still been a prolonged period to support yourself on small or no income.

65 is the traditional retirement age, but it continues to change as more Americans find that they cannot float more than 20 years of living without a paycheck. 20% of Americans age 65 and older still works and about half of those who are still working are motivated by their financial problems. If you can afford to retire when you want to, then it is a luxury.

You see money as your ally

Most people have an adversaries and dysfunctional relationship with money. After all, people are taught that money is scarce, which is difficult to earn, but more difficult to keep. If you want to start attracting money, you should stop seeing it as your enemy. Rather, you should think of this as one of your greatest allies.

The reason behind why rich people are earning even more wealth is because they are not scared of admitting that money is able to solve most problems. People in middle class sees money as a never-ending significant even that you have to endure as part of life. On the other hand, the world class views money as a great liberator, and when you have enough of it, you can buy financial peace of mind. If you are not afraid of money, and if you see it as your ally and tool that can help you in attaining what you want in life, you now know for yourself that you are rich.

You can pay for the things that you really want.

If you can go out purchasing a yacht in cash today, most people will agree that you are wealth. On the other hand, if you are able to go out purchasing that same yacht after five years and after you have set a savings goal, socking away money every month or year. You are most probably still wealthy.

Americans do not save all that much. Around 33% of respondents do not have household savings, and there are thousands of Americans found that 1/3 of them do not have any retirement savings or plans.

You are not stuck

Through time, rich people have realized that in different ways, money means freedom. If you can control your finances, you will not find yourself stuck in places, relationships, or jobs that you hate only because you cannot afford to go on other places. To be in a good place financially may open up lots of doors. On the other hand, being in a bad spot will be able to slam them in your face.

Chapter 2: What is the Science of Getting Rich?

The science of getting rich all come back to one simple equation. As soon as you understand the equation and know how to use it in manifesting anything that you want, you can guarantee success. Every piece of this important equation of getting rich is easy to understand of and in itself. However, it is only when they are all put together in the right way that you will have unlimited success.

Results

Result is what all of us want. It is what we always hope for and dream of. If you put the complete equation into effect, the results that you would get are the results you want. The key before you go into the other parts of the equation is that you should take time to be clear on the results that you want to have. If you want to get rich faster and easier, you must have a clear image of what it exactly means to you. What does it mean to get rich easily and quickly? What would you have if you were rich? Where would you live? What would you own? How much is rich for you? There are lots of questions in your mind.

When you get a clear understanding about the results that you want, it is important to be as accurate as possible. The more accurate you are, the easier it is going to be to manifest the results you desire. In line with this, you should know the picture of the exact house you want, the exact colors of cars, the exact amount of money that you want as your income every month, among others. The more accurate you become in every detail, the more effect and the easier it will be to implement the manifestation equation.

Actions

Action is what people think as the most essential in becoming rich. Most people believe that it may happen if you would just work around 20 hours per day and tirelessly work until it happens. It is a fact that taking action is essential for success, but you may hurt your how effective you are if you take the wrong actions. To get the results that you want, it is very important to put in action, but you cannot know if they are the correct actions until you become as precise as possible and understand the results you want.

Furthermore, it is significant to be on your desired results, as you can ensure that you would take the right and appropriate actions to be able to get there. When you understand the results that you want and become accurate in it, and it is time for you to take action, make sure that each action you take will lead you to specific results.

Feelings

To be able to take the correct actions that you need so as to connect with what you emotionally want. You need to experience what it's like to have what you want in a core emotional level. Feel the experience of driving that car, sleeping in the bed at your new home, and more. Experiencing things in an emotional level is the commonly-overlooked key in manifesting your desires in life. These feelings are a priority but they are not where things start. Things start without thoughts, and then lead to our feelings.

Thoughts

This is where all the manifestation success starts. It is important to have your thoughts in appropriate alignment with the results you want to be able to become successful. The biggest danger to your success is to enable the wrong thoughts in. You need to focus your mind on the right thoughts all the time. Furthermore, you would want to make sure that each though you have will be positive into your goals. Occasionally, you may find yourself having negative thoughts that might pop up. This is normal, and what matters is about how you react to them. We all have that occasional negative thought time, but it is very important to select ways on how you can react quickly by deciding to stop the thought tracks and replace it with a present and positive thought, aligned with the results you desire.

When you bring these sciences to get rich, you will have the secret to being rich and sure success. Start by ensuring that all your thoughts will be the right present, positive, and right thoughts in alignment with the results you desire. As soon as your thoughts are formed correctly, then you will be able to start feeling these thoughts on an emotional level. As soon as you know how it feels to have these thoughts as a reality, you will know what actions you should take in order to make these feelings of you a reality. Take actions every day and you will end up with results that you have always wanted. It is as simple as this.

Chapter 3: 8 Money Mistakes to Avoid on your Way to Getting Rich

The rich people avoid the mistakes that huge income earners make. The following are some of the common money handling mistakes that must be avoided to create wealth.

1. **Diversification** – You will never be able to get rich by diversifying your investments. Diversification is like putting all your eggs in one basket and then watching that basket. If you really want to be rich, you should learn everything you can with regards to a space and go all in.

2. **Investing in trends** – You should avoid investing in greatest and latest technologies, which may be exiled by the new developments in technology. Do not get on the roller coaster. It is highly recommended to take the slower and longer ride, but guarantees your arrival.

3. **Pretender spender** – There will always be a pretender spender in the spectrum. On the other hand, it is greater to impress other with how they spend money. It is not their money. It will always be someone else's money. There are shoes, expensive clothes, sports cars, VIP tables, designer bags, and more. The list is endless. True rich people are not trying hard to impress anyone, they're seeking freedom.

4. **Seeking comfort, instead of freedom** – Comfort is the most dangerous element of finances, and is the enemy of abundance. The whole middle class has been built to seek comfort. The rich people seek freedom and abundance that money is not anymore dependent on their efforts. More is the mantra. Then, abundance has been the affirmation, with comfort not being on their menu. Freedom is the focus.

5. **Comparing to others** – Around 76% of working US citizens live from one paycheck to another. When you compare your finances to others, you are never going to create wealth. Most commonly, people are comparing their current situation to some of the starving country in a remote corner of the world so as to justify being much better off. In other person's finances, no matter if it is bad or good, will no pay your bills. It will not fund your retirement and it will not be providing peace of mind to you. Do not compare your finances to others.

6. **Saving to save** – It is not possible to make true richness by just saving money. The banks only pay 0.25%, so it will take you about 40 years in order to grow your money by 10% - this is if the rates do not change. More significantly, money that sits around inactive always seems to look for ways for emergency funding. Do not carry credit cards or cash because you will always have a reason to use it when either is available. To guarantee your wealth, you may move your saved money into the future accounts for investments which you will not be able to have access to easily. In this way, money will be available

for investments when you finally had the courage and knowledge to do so. This will keep you broke, resulting to hustle consistently.

7. **Depending on one income flow** – Regardless of how big your income is, it is important to not depend on one flow. Assuming you are an executive who earns around 300,000 every year, which is the top percent of all incomes. But the industry you are working at suddenly came to stop, meaning, your single income flow was halted or shut-down. This happened to lots of Americans, and destroying around trillion dollars of pretended richness. To be able to make wealth, you need to create investments that are going to make dependable income streams, independent of your primary source of income. You may consider rental income from apartments and apartments in other companies so as to throw off the passive income flows.

8. **Trusting without proof** – The one greatest mistake that you can face in your financial life is trusting people naively because you liked them and because it felt right. You neglected to get a proof that these people were actually as what they presented. Rather, you went with your feelings and then was deceived. By the time that you figured out that there is something wrong, you were out millions. When it comes to people, you should disregard your feelings, and it is important to always look for solid evidence. If you are very close to people to the point that you become not willing to ask them for evidence, better make it a policy to not do business with them.

When the rich people hit abundance and affluence, they start to throw money around on ridiculous things, such as planes, cars, vacation home, and boats. It then not matters anymore that things are poor investments. The rich people may look like they have been showing their money with much extravagances, but they are not. The money that they spend is minuscule than the abundance that they have made.

Money will not make you happy and just getting by will not either. There will be a price to be paid for any choices you made. Wealth is providing options to you, and those who have options have freedom.

Chapter 4: 3 Warning Signs on How to Get Wealthy

All small businesses always look for answers to the question, "how to get wealthy?". Hence, they are consistently on the lookout to expand. Now, many times, their schemes are working out, but in most cases, people just end up making mistakes with disastrous consequences. This is for the reason that most people did not managed to perfect the art of reading all the warning signs about their business being in trouble. Experience is something that cannot be measured, but if you want to get rich, you do not have the benefit of it.

1. **Rapid Growth** – You are probably having trouble believing your eyes on your business. If your growth is too rapid, chances are that you do not have adequate infrastructure and you are playing a game that is just going to make your business vulnerable. Rather than answering how to get rich successfully, you may actually be planning about your downfall. For instance, if you are venturing out of your target market, you might just run into trouble because the demands of people, together with their purchasing potentials are starkly different. This will lead you to losing out and this mean, losing out bad.

2. **Money Matters** – All good businessmen are knowledgeable that they are stepping on egg shells with a big load on the back, if the funds are very limited that they are having trouble to cough up the daily expenditure like bills and others. Among the greatest ways to make assessment whether your business is in trouble is when you are producing finance with debt instead of with equity. This is a necessity in the Operation: How to Get Rich. Aside from that, if it takes too long to recognize that your customers have debt from you, together with the additional fact that your sales are dwindling and you have increasing expenses, you know that your company will be in troubled waters. If you want to know how to get rich, you will need to think first of a way out of this situation.

3. **Straying** – Many times, entrepreneurs decide to venture in an unknown territory, lured by success stories. They most commonly do not know too much about their new venture. So, rather than concentrating on their core products, they begin to concentrate on ancillaries. However, they did not realize that customers are patronizing their because due to their primary product. In line with this, it would be a stupid decision to let go of that. If you find yourself straying, you must make sure that you recognize it as a warning sign. It will not tell you how to get rich, but it will make you lose out on funds.

Every entrepreneur wants to make it huge in life and because of this, they have unwittingly been making mistakes. You will need to learn how to get rich by keeping in mind these warning signs. This is because you would want to keep the money that you are making.

Chapter 5: Smart and Effective Ways to be Wealthy

Almost everyone wants wealth, but only few know what they must do to be able to get it. To be wealthy takes a combination of skill, luck, and patience, and you will have to set yourself on a way that leads you to a money enriching career, then handle your earned money by saving it, investing it, and decreasing your living expenses. It is not easy to get rich, but with a skillful decision making and a little perseverance, it is ultimately possible.

a. **Investment**

Among the greatest investment in life is saving money for retirement. Just keep saving. There are seemingly fewer people who adequately save for retirement. There are some people who may never be able to get to retire. Take advantage of the retirement plans that are tax-deferred like 401K and IRA. Their embodied tax treatment will be helpful for you in saving quicker for retirement. Consider investment in a Roth IRA – a retirement account where working people may contribute around $5,500 yearly. Then, that money is invested and it gathers compound interest. If you wait until your retirement age to be able to take money out of your Roth IRA, your withdrawn money will not be taxed because it has been taxed during the time you earned it first.

Also, you should not put all your trust to the social security. Although it is a good thing to invest in the social security, it will continue working for the next 20 years or so, if the Congress does not alter the system radically (either by decreasing benefits or raising taxes), social security will not become available in its current form. However, there is a possibility that the Congress would act to fix this. In any event, the social security has never been designed to be the only source for retiring people in their later years. This is why you should save and invest for the future.

Contributing to a 401K account is another great idea. Your employer will be the one to set up this account in which pre-taxed contributions can be invested. Your employer could select all or some parts of your contributions. This is possibly the closest thing that you will get in order to have free money in your life. To take advantage of the match, contribute at least enough. Don't do purchases that are likely to rapidly depreciate. It is, at times, considered a waste to spend 50,000 dollars on a car because it is very likely that it will not be worth half that much in 5 years, no matter how much work you put to it. As soon as you drive off a new car, it will be depreciating around 20 to 25% in value and it will continue to do so every year you own it. This makes purchasing a car a very significant financial decision.

Aside from that, you should consider putting money in the stock market. Invest money in bonds, stocks, or other vehicles of investment that will give you a yearly ROI that is great enough to sustain you for retirement. For example, if you a million dollar invest and get a reliable 7% ROI, you will get 70,000 dollars every year, with less inflation. Do not get enticed by day traders who always say that it is easy to make money easily. Purchasing and selling dozens of stocks daily is significantly gambling. If you are going to make some bad trades, you will be losing so much money and it is not a great way to get rich. On the other hand, you should learn to invest for the long run. Select great stocks that have outstanding leadership and solid fundamentals in industries that are primed for great growth in the future. Then, do not do anything with your stock; let it sit and let it weather the ups and downs. You should do well through time if you invest wisely.

Another NO in investing and getting rich is not to spend money on stupid stuff. It is difficult enough to make a living, but it is more difficult and painful when the things you spend your hard-earned cash on are black holes in your financial life. Evaluate again the things you spend your money on. Try figuring out whether or not they are worth it. There are several things that you possibly do not want to spend much money on if you are planning to become rich:

- **Vices**. One example is cigarettes. Heavy smokers are only watching their money go up in smoke.

- **First-class plane tickets**. What will you get for that extra 1,000 dollars? Another 4-inches of leg room and a hot towel? You should rather invest that money than throwing it away.

- **Huge markups**. This includes drinks at a club or candy at the movie theater.

- **Lottery tickets and casinos**. Very few lucky people make money in casinos and lottery tickets. The rest of us lose it.

- **Plastic surgery and tanning booths**. You may get free skin cancer outside if you want. Also, do Botox injections and nose jobs ever look as good as promised? You should learn how to age gracefully; you are not the only one who gets older.

While investing to get rich, you should include your time in your investment. For instance, you might like having free time, so you give yourself several hours per day doing nothing. However, if you plan to invest your several hours to get rich, you might work into having 20 years of free time with early retirement. And while doing so, consider investing in real estate. Stable assets like potential development land or rental properties, in a steadily growing area is a great way of building wealth. There are no guarantees in any investment but many people have done well with real estate investment. These kinds of investment appreciate in value through time. For instance, there are people who think that an apartment in Manhattan is nearly guaranteed to be able to increase in value over any period of 5 years.

It is difficult to get rich, but it is even more difficult to stay rich. Your richness will always be affected by the market, and the market has ups and downs. When times are good and you become too comfortable, you will quickly drop back to the very beginning when the market hits a slump. If your ROI goes up a percentage point, or you get a raise or promotion, do not spend the extra. Save it for when the business is slow and your ROI goes down.

b. Career enrichment

Select the right profession. Look at surveys of salary which determine the average yearly incomes for particular professions. Your odds to get rich will be diminished if you pursue a career in teaching as contrary to a career in finance. Here are some of the highest paying jobs in the US.

- **Software engineers and IT managers.** If you are a whiz at computers and good at programming, consider this well-compensated field. IT managers are regularly making a hundred thousand dollars every year.

- **Surgeons and doctors.** Anesthesiologists are making more than 200,000 dollars every year.

- **Lawyers.** Attorneys top out at just about 130,000 dollars every year, which makes it a lucrative field if you are able to put in the time.

- **Petroleum engineers.** The engineers who are working with oil and gas companies are able to make a good living. In many cases, they are able to make more than 135,000 dollars every year.

But first of all, before you plan to get rich through a career enrichment, it is important to excel academically. Regardless if it is a vocational training or a 4-year college, some successful people are pursuing further education above high school. In the early stages of your career, your employers will have little by which to judge you aside from your educational background. When you have higher grades, you will have higher salaries. In line with this, it is recommended to get an entry-level job and work your way up. Apply to different places and subject yourself to many interviews. When you get your job, stick with it and get the experience you need in order to advance.

Select the right location. Go where the good jobs are. Like for instance, if you desire to pursue finance, you can get greater opportunities in big cities as compared to low-populated rural areas. On the other hand, if you are planning to build a startup, you would want to consider going to Silicon Valley. If you want to pursue your career in the entertainment industry, go to New York City or Los Angeles. Furthermore, change employer and jobs. As soon as you have gotten some experience under your belt, you should find a new job. When you change your environment, you will be able to increase your pay and you can experience various corporate cultures. Do not be scared to do this several times. If you are a valued employee, your current company may offer a raise to you or other benefits if they know that you are leaving.

c. Living Expenses Reduction

Purchase in bulk. It is not the easiest way to shop, but it is commonly the most efficient. If you are able to borrow or purchase into a membership to a bulk retailer, it can make real financial sense. In several cases, you can find brand-name products for sale at serious discounts. If you are hungry and you like chicken, you should purchase chickens at the end of the day when they go on sale. At times, they will drop in half, which means that you will be able to get at least 10 hearty meals for half of the original price. You can freeze any chickens that you are not eating immediately.

Reduce your utility bills. Gas, electricity, and other utilities may impact your monthly budget deeply if you let them. Be smart about different ways to keep your home warm during winter and cool during the summer. You can even consider building or investing in solar panels to channel the natural energy from the sun into electricity. When you keep your utilities low, you can watch the money you save starting to mount. You may also try extreme couponing. It is among the best feelings in the world when you get paid on the things that you use regularly. If you do it right, you can get paid to using a coupon. At worst, you will be able to save a few moneys that you can possibly tuck away during the rainy season. At best, you will be able to get lots of free stuff and get richer during the process.

Get a home energy audit. This will enable you to find out how many dollars have been seeping out of your home in the form of lost energy. You may perform your own audit on your energy consumption if you are an industrious type, but do not hesitate to hire an expert to complete the task for you. It should cost hundreds of dollars, which is relatively not cheap, but it may be helpful to you in saving much more than what it cost you, through time, most particularly if you are planning to re-insulate your home.

Learn to can your foods. About 40% of foods in the US goes to waste before it is even eaten. Blueberries, succulent peaches, and even meats may be stored and canned for future consumption. Be smart about the foods you purchase. You should really eat it. Wasted food is wasted money. On the other hand, you may consider go foraging or hunting for food. You may have to invest in permits and gear, but if you already have these things, this will be an inexpensive way of getting your own food. If you are against animal killing, it is very easy to forage for food, depending on where you live. Just ensure that you are foraging only for foods whose properties and origin you are sure of. Getting poisoned or sick is never fun. Go fishing or fly fishing, go duck hunting, deer hunting, or turkey hunting, build your own greenhouse or start guerrilla gardening, or pick wild mushrooms, choose edible flowers, or forage for food in the Fall.

d. **Saving Money**

Make a budget and stick to it. Make a budget for each month that covers all your basic expenses and leaves some fun money aside. Saving money even a little per month and sticking to your budget is a good way of laying the groundwork for your efforts to get wealthy. Pay yourself first. Before you go blowing your paycheck on a golf club and a new pair of shoes that you don't need, put that money aside in an account that you are not touching. Do this each time you get paid and watch your account growing. Another thing to do if you want to save money is basically to cut your expenses. Look at the ways how you spend money frivolously and think of everything again. For instance, avoid going to

Starbucks each morning. That 4 dollars that you are spending on a designer coffee each morning comes out to 28 dollars every week, and a thousand dollar in a year.

Spend your tax refund wisely. The average tax refund in America is about 3,000 dollars and that is a lot of money. You can make an emergency fund or pay off debts with that rather than blowing it on something that will lose half of its value as soon as you purchase it. If you invest your 3,000 dollars wisely, it might be worth 10x that much in as many years. Downgrade your house and car. Will you save more with an apartment rather than a house, or have roommates rather than your own place? Will you be able to purchase a used car rather than a new one and use it more sparingly? There are only some of many ways to save lots of money per month.

Track your expenses down. In order to soar your effectiveness on cutting your expenses, it is important that you keep track of them. Choose one of the several expense tracking applications that are around, and record each penny that goes in and out of your wallet. After three months of so, you will know where most of your money go and about what you can do for that. Also, it is time for you to break up with your credit card. Did you know that people using credit cards for buying things end up spending more money as compared to people who use cash? This is because parting with cash is very painful. Using a credit card will not carry that much of a sting. Break up with your credit card and see how it feels to pay with cash, you may end up saving a lot.

On the other hand, if you can maintain a credit card, do things to decrease your expenses. Try paying off the full balance on time and every month. This will lead to an interest-free credit. At the very least, you can make the month-to-month minimum payment before the due date in order to avoid having a late fee.

e. Going Mortgage Free

You should refinance your home mortgage, and consider refinancing it to a lower rate or to a 25-year loan rather than a 30-year loan. With this, you will only be paying some extra hundred dollars every month but you can save yourself much more than that in total interest. The interest that you are paying each month will be reduced to 60x because you will only be paying your loan for 25 years instead of 30 years. That is 60 months free of monthly expenses and interest.

Chapter 6: Why Getting Rich is Easier than you Think?

Many people are chasing success by working hard and sacrificing their social and personal lives. They are pushing themselves so hard that they may end up with health problems related to stress because of their relentless pursuit of wealth. But it does not need to be this way. Look for opportunities or a gap in the market that you can take advantage of.

Stop your self-limiting beliefs. Most people have doubt on themselves and because of this, they are setting their eyes in the middle, not too high but not too low too. This is how people think and so the competition in the middle has been very high. This is the reason why you should think big and aim big. There will be less competition here and you may even find that thinking big will result to a place where things really happen. Have an unwavering self-belief. Passion, belief in your capabilities, persistence, and ideas will get you far. Now is the right time to live your dreams.

Know what your strengths and weaknesses. Know what you are good at and capitalize on your strengths, and minimize your weaknesses. They will only become a problem if you allow them to be. Do not be scared of failing. See the process of trial and error as a positive way forward. Outsource what you are specifically not good at. Do not waste your time to try doing and being everything. Furthermore, surround yourself with people who are positive and who have similar interests. Expand your social network with websites like LinkedIn and Meetup. The connections may create a big difference to the failure or success of a project. It is commonly your credentials as an expert that wins the day, but your personality and how you can connect with people. If they like you, you will have more possibility of winning the business.

Conclusion

The first route to getting rich is to discover yourself, along with your different talents and the strengths you have. You should also take advantage of your weaknesses to improve and discover yourself further. Knowing yourself is part of the process to identify which are the best opportunities at the right time so that you can reach your goals to become rich effectively. If you have good talents that you think have many potentials, do not hide them. Rather, you should cultivate them and turn yourself into a mast of your own craft. If you are aware of your real talents, you are going to have ease in selecting what you really want to do, so that you can reach your goals in life.

Set your goals, both short term and long term. Having goals in life is important if you want to attain sure financial success because these will serve to provide you direction. Keep in mind that when you set goals, you will have to ensure that they are realistic and can be attained or else, you will just end up frustrating yourself in the end. When you have everything properly organized through guides from this book, you can start your own business effectively, and having your own business is among the most surefire ways to become rich.

Jason Mark

Also, Check Out This Other Book Published by Success Publishing

Automatic Income Machines

Free Preview Bonus

Automatic Income Machines: e-Business Blueprint

With an economic whiplash that hits most the countries today; more people are joining ranks in achieving economic progress through the internet. The internet world had become an American Dream while others look at it as the other side of the world with the greener pasture.

Many had indeed taken their chance in starting an online business, yet not all are ready to face all the challenges and the complexities of surviving in the internet business arena.

However, for those who were lucky enough to survive, they lived to testify to the kind of life online business offers.

This "e-Business Blueprint" aims to provide beginners with a guide on setting up an online business and guiding you through the simple steps to achieve success.

With proper knowledge and determination, success on any online business can be achievable and in fact, rewarding. It's just a matter of planning and driving you towards a goal that can really make your dream comes true.

CHAPTER 1: Reasons for Getting Into an Online

Business

People got different reasons for going into online business. But most often, online business is for people who got tired of working 8-5 or 9-6 every day. Rushing each morning for a gulp of coffee before fighting his way through traffic and hoping he could be earlier than usual!

As you realized that you are getting tired of working for someone else and you want to become your own boss, you start thinking of the possibility to make it big in the internet business. Hoping, you are right, and then the best way to set up a business with a greater chance to make it to success is to start now!

Here are just a few of the many reasons why you must start with your internet business.

Goodbye to Traffic and Early Morning Rush

With an internet business, you don't need to rush up too early that you need to skip eating breakfast just so you can arrive in time for work. But when you are living in an overcrowded metropolis where you had to go through jam-packed traffic, stress and anxiety can be a daily part of your routine!

Online business can help you save a lot of money by not traveling every day. Count the savings you can have when you don't need to go out for work. You can likewise save your time and convert the time spent for daily trips into more productive inputs.

No Need Putting Up with a Toxic Boss

Most often people got fed up and want to get out of their work because they have a toxic person for a boss. Most often, bosses thought that their employees are there to please them all the time. This often happens when you are working in a sole proprietorship type of business or a one-man organization. Most often than not, you feed to your boss whims and schemes rather than get productive in your tasks. In the end, you feel thoroughly burnt out and find a quick way to change job.

Working at your own Pace and Time

When you are running an online business, you can be your own boss. You can work at a chosen time and place. You can even have more time to yourself and to your family. However, this can have its own drawback. So, before you get out of your work, be sure your finances or the lack of will not cripple you. Proper timing is needed so your family will not suffer from your decision.

When you are free to decide for yourself whether you are going to work or not, be sure you manage your time effectively and efficiently. When you're alone to manage your time and no one is around to put pressure on you, you don't give yourself a reason to procrastinate. You need to learn to balance everything even without someone to answer to. Remember that every minute wasted is an opportunity lost in online business.

Unlimited Income Potential

Working on a regular career means putting up a cap on how much you can earn. But with online business, your ability to earn depends on how much time you want to put into your business. You can earn as much or as little as you want. The market for online business is too vast. You just learn to tap its unlimited resources and you go as far as you can.

You can target people around the world as the global market is getting bigger and bigger and more people are learning how to access the internet every day. You can work as much or as little as you choose. The marketplace for internet businesses is worldwide.

Per the later report of the Statistics portal, the number of internet users had risen up to 3.17 billion this year from 2.94 of the previous year. Doesn't that market large enough to dip your toes into?

Minimal Expenses for an Office

Since you are working from the comfort of your home, you don't need to rent an office space. You will again be saving a lot on your administrative expenses compared if you are running a conventional type of business.

In setting up your business, all you need to have is your laptop or PC and low-cost hardware and software which you can even get for free online if you're just diligent enough to browse through your internet.

Bigger Chance to Achieve more for Less Work

An online business allows you to work fewer hours and achieve more. There are some business models that can be fully automated. You just must set them up and (lo!), they can run on their own and earns you a passive income. This automation process now is widely used in the internet market. If you can't run your business on 100% automation, you can at least have it automated at 50% or more, so you can have more time for additional business to carry on.

What makes an online business unique than conventional ones is you can operate multiple businesses single-handedly. To simplify, you are operating a business that is almost next to impossible – Less capital, less time, and less effort for unlimited income streams potentials.

Common Problems you will Encounter at the Start of your Online Business

Starting your online business can be both rewarding and stimulating. However, you are sure to encounter a few problems that new entrepreneurs usually encounter. To steer clear of these issues, you must be aware of them and avoid them as they come along.

Tempting Opportunities and Resources

As you start hanging on the internet, you will be meeting a lot of opportunities along with remarkable resources to promising you great support in your online business. These products, usually software or a business opportunity, may be as great as their vendor advertise them. Nonetheless, if you jump from one opportunity to another, you will be losing your focus on your core business. It is, therefore, important that you start an online business with only what you absolutely need and have it run smoothly before getting into another. The same works with your software or any other tool.

Neglecting New Opportunities

Basically, this is the exact opposite of grabbing every opportunity that comes along. If you refuse to examine or look at any new opportunity sent your way because you have your focus set up trying to achieve a goal with a method that simply don't work, avoid overlooking the warning signs that tell you that you need to move on or move in another direction.

Doing Everything by Yourself

When you think it's better to keep all the profit, you keep trying to do everything so you can keep the money to yourself. Saving is always good for your business, but as your business develops, it will become impossible for you to embrace all the tasks. This is the time when you need to develop some way to ease up your workload. An example of these if subscribing for an auto responder that will take care of your mailing activities. Instead of manually sending letters, answering queries, the auto-responder allows you to maintain and develop relationships with your customer base and up-sell or cross-sell your products and services.

Having Too Many Choices

Affiliate marketing is a good start for an online business for you can earn as soon as someone buys from your inks. This is the reason why it is so popular with many people. Affiliate marketing method has many positive aspects but there are too many choices that it is confusing to know which to promote. Before you jump into marketing a new software by way of an affiliate program, check how much commission you can earn from it, how you can get paid, and know if there is some support you can get from the owner. It is also important to know if the product sells before promoting it.

The Internet is Bigger than What You Think

Having an online business doesn't mean that people will naturally visit your website and buy things that you offer. The internet is such an enormous marketplace that you need to know how to get prospective customers to visit your visit so you can have the chance to convert these visits into sales. Meaning, you need to learn how to generate website traffic by utilizing both free and paid traffic generators.

No Support from Family and Friend

Sometimes, we presume that our family and friends will be our loyal customer. Sad to say, in most cases, it doesn't usually happen especially during the start of your business. There are even cases when they will discourage you from doing online business. Though these people mean well, don't get easily swayed and let your goals and efforts get destructed. If you have set your goal and created a business plan to back it up, you have every opportunity to get successful.

Regardless of whom you are, your age, gender, technical skills, educational background, you can always start your own internet business. You can always harness whatever skill you have through various learning platforms and resources provided on the internet for a certain fee or for free.

DOWNLOAD Automatic Income Machines NOW!

www.ingramcontent.com/pod-product-compliance
Lightning Source LLC
Chambersburg PA
CBHW081320180526
45170CB00007B/2789